Books by Stan Rosenzweig

Smart Selling How You Can Turn Ordinary Selling Into Extraordinary Income. Twenty lessons that have helped thousands to earn millions.

Smart Marketing What Big Companies Practice And You Must Learn About Positioning, Branding And Other Marketing Concepts.

Smart Telemarketing How You Can Turn Ordinary Telemarketing Into Extraordinary Income.

Smart Sales Management How You Can Use The Powerful Lessons Of Others To Help You To Build And Lead A Winning Sales And Management Team.

Smart Thinking How To Use Your Own Life Experiences To Reach Greater Success. Chicken soup may be good, but front line sales experience is better.

Sailing For Non-Sailors What Every Guest Should Know Before Stepping Aboard.

Hotel Telecommunications Opportunities Through Deregulation.

Smart Telemarketing

· · · · · · · · · · · · · · · · · · ·

How You Can Turn
Ordinary Telemarketing
Into Extraordinary
Income

Stan Rosenzweig

PRINTED IN THE UNITED STATES OF AMERICA

ISBN 1-58652-000-8

Publisher's Cataloging-in-Publication
(Provided by Quality Books, Inc.)

Rosenzweig, Stan.
Smart telemarketing : how you can turn ordinary
   telemarketing into extraordinary income / Stan
Rosenzweig. – 1st ed.
     p. cm.
     ISBN 1-58652-001-6
     "LCCN: 99-75934"

1. Telemarketing.   I. Title

HF5415.1265.R67 2000   658.8´4
            QBI99-1551

Table of Contents

How to get the most
from this training course

*T*his self-paced training includes plenty of good advice to make you more successful at sales. It will help you to be more productive selling your products and services. It will help you to make more money and will help you enjoy your success.

How do I know? For one thing, I have been training sales people and sales teams for more than 25 years. I started out as an AT&T telemarketing trainer back before MCI decided to break up the phone monopoly and when every long distance phone call resulted in AT&T revenue. Our simple goal: get businesses to phone more often.

As AT&T PhonePower ™ trainers, we would go out to visit manufacturers, truck sales companies, anyone who sold stuff, and we would teach them how to do it better over the phone... and it worked. Our customers sold more using our training assistance, so they were willing to make more phone calls. Eventually, our customers were able to create so many leads that they needed to learn how to complete the sales cycle and close more deals. So we accepted that challenge to train them in all steps of the sale.

Since then, I have helped tens of thousands of business people through seminars, books and magazine columns, including 120 sales and marketing training columns for a very popular sales publication, Reseller Management Magazine. Readers have sent me an amazing number of letters of thanks over the years, so I know that the material I have prepared for you, here, will work.

In customizing the information in this training on selling so that it helps you to sell more, I have relied on more than years of sales training experience. I interviewed hundreds of sales people, some successful and some not so, in order to determine what sales problems you are facing in the field. I interviewed numerous people who need to sell but have no training, people who are wonderful on the technical side, but who have important questions regarding how best to increase sales.

You told me you would love to learn:
1. How to uncover greater numbers of fresh sales leads.
2. How to overcome fears prospects have regarding reliability and trust.
3. How to organize your sales calls to greatest effect.
4. How to stand up to competition from large, traditional vendors.

The 80/20 rule is wonderful when applied to sales training. It says that you derive 80% of benefit in the first 20%

of the time and the remaining 20% of benefit in the remaining 80% of the time. I don't know if that is 100% true, but this sales training resource will answer your most urgent sales questions and will provide you with tools to make more sales.

80/20 notwithstanding, if you have had no prior selling experience, or if your current sales results are limited, you should consider this as a great beginning to build on, a valuable resource, but not the only resource. Read additional books and magazines on sales and marketing. Attend selling seminars. Join groups and associations comprised of sales professionals who freely exchange ideas leading to greater success.

Recognize that selling is a profession that gives forth its greatest rewards to those who continue to expand their professional understanding with time set aside, each month, to invest in its study. For those of us who do, it's a wonderful way to succeed. So, let's turn directly to Lesson One and start creating more fresh sales leads.

Four points that mean the difference between telemarketing success and failure.

*T*elephone canvassing, or cold calling, is the practice of sitting down with a long list of potential prospects you've never met and telephoning them, one at a time, to learn which of them needs what you sell and then arranging to sell it to them. Nobody likes telephone cold calling.

Salesmen don't like it because they perceive that cold calls are to unfriendly, unkind strangers who would rather see you in a one-on-one with Hulk Hogan than see you in their offices. It's true. They are. They would.

Prospects don't always like cold calls because they are from people they don't know, asking questions they don't want to discuss. These calls are unscheduled, intrusive and sometimes can be a general pain in the South Forty. (For those few prospects who would love to tell telemarketing folks off, I suggest a new service: 1(900) TRASH EM. One dollar per minute. Parental consent required.) At other times, however, prospects DO respond well to cold calls, open up freely and give us the chance to sell what they need.

So, here's the dilemma, if we don't like doing it, and prospects don't always know when they like it done to them, why is it that we ALL need to make cold phone calls part of our selling strategy? Here are only a few reasons:

- It's the fastest way to qualify prospects.
- It lets them know what we do.
- It's targeted. It's the best way to learn who the decision maker is.
- It creates a personal relationship with the buyer.
- It keeps us productive when store traffic is down.
- It reaches prospects we miss in other activities.

While telephone canvassing is considered basic, some do much better at it than others. If you would like to make the best use of your telemarketing time, here are four key points to make you a telemarketing leader.

POINT 1. 80% OF THE SALE IS TALKING TO THE RIGHT PERSON.

In face to face selling, everybody knows how to qualify the right buyer. You always try to get to the key decision maker. Of course, you know this. Everybody knows this. But when we phone a strange new number, unfortunately, we don't practice the basics and fail to face our fear of being rejected by a faceless voice, so, too often, we end up presenting to the person who cannot buy.

Many of you ask the receptionist, "Who handles your computer purchases (software purchases, telephone purchases, etc.?)" This doesn't work. You must stop worrying about failure and start concentrating on talking to more people who buy. When you speak to the receptionist ask, "Can you tell me who the Controller or Vice President of Finance is?"

This is very important, because the Vice President of Finance or Controller, is usually the person most likely to either listen to what you have to say or refer you to the appropriate party. Do not ask, "Who handles your computers?" The person who handles the computer could be the order entry clerk, or the bookkeeper, or the facilities manager, or the purchasing agent who buys paper clips and note pads, or the personnel manager.

All of these people have the authority to turn you down, but none of them have the authority to meet with you to accept your proposal and start using your services. The exception is when a higher officer refers you to one of these people, because this person is then given the authority to buy. Plus, you have the option of going back to the person you originally spoke to once before.

If the company does not have a Controller or Vice President of Finance, ask next to speak to the President, because a company without these critical financial officers is very small and the President is usually the owner and key decision maker. Here, again, the owner can refer you down the line, but it is almost impossible to be referred up the line if you start at a lower level.

You know these are the basics of selling, but we all sometimes forget them. If your appointment success rate is very low, consider this first point, that you may not be canvassing the right people.

POINT 2. AFTER THE OPENING REMARKS, STOP TELLING AND START ASKING.

They say that the first 20 seconds of every phone call is most critical and you have to say something interesting enough to keep the prospect on the line for the rest of the call. True, but then what? The most productive use of your time is to ask questions to learn where you can fit in.

Here is how I would do it: "Hi. My name is Stan Rosenzweig with Office Technology Consulting. We provide computer networking and telecommunications solutions to the financial and business community. We have testimonials from all across America that our solutions are the most cost effective you can find. May I ask you a few questions to see if we can benefit your business?"

If you notice, there are four components to this opener that are all covered in this very short span of time (actually timed at 18 seconds):

1. A very brief, but complete, introduction.
2. A very brief description of what we do.
3. A strong reason for the prospect to stay on the phone.
4. A segue into a Q & A session that gets the prospect involved in the process and helps us both determine if this call is worthwhile.

If this kind of twenty second intro gets you to the next part of the call, you can relax a bit and start asking about the prospect's plans to buy whatever it is you sell, to determine if the prospect has problems you can solve, or – most importantly, if that's your goal – to set up a meeting.

Focus your questions on two areas:
- Problems he or she needs to solve in a cost effective way.
- Solutions you sell that will solve his or her problems.

If you find a problem/solution mix, you will reap these benefits:
- He or she will recognize the benefits of a visit with you.
- You will see the benefits of a visit, also – you will have a QUALIFIED lead.

At this point, you are a success. Make an appointment to see him and don't bother to read the rest of this lesson. If you are not yet a success, read on.

POINT 3. KNOW WHEN TO TALK. KNOW WHEN TO LISTEN. KNOW WHEN TO CLOSE.

Selling is not an art. It's a craft that you learn through study and practice. So is telemarketing. The best way to learn telemarketing is under the personal tutelage of a master... your own personal marketing Yoda. Second best is by reading what many masters have written.

In addition to this book, you will find that a trip to the local bookstore's business and management section will reveal dozens of good guides to this craft. Choose more than one, or two, and read them several times. For the most part, you will find that it's a matter of personal style and taste. Browse until you find the ones with the style you like best (Also, if you are web-enabled, visit www.salestipwebsite.com where we plan to review various quality training products from time to time).

I have given this advice many, many times over the years and there are many successful telemarketers who have come back to thank me for it. Knowing who to speak to, asking instead of telling and improving your telemarketing education are all very important, but the fourth point may be most important of all and it has more to do with life in general than it has to do with selling.

POINT 4. DO NOT TRY TO BE PERFECT. LEARN FROM YOUR MISTAKES AND PROMPTLY MOVE ON.

Someone recently said to me, in a gathering, "Perfectionism is the greatest form of self abuse!" Wow! It sure is true, isn't it? We all spend too much time reviewing how we could have done it, should have done it, would have done it, if only we were smarter, faster, more careful, less in a hurry, and on and on .

You can't inventory the past. Airlines and hotel companies know that yesterday's seats and rooms are gone. So, too, with yesterday's mistakes. If you drag them around with you, you become depressed and depression is one of a salesman's worst enemies.

If you have gained from the first three points, great. Now, let go of the past. Instead of cultivating perfectionism for perfection's sake, defined by some as "the greatest form of self-abuse," work on having a better, more productive today. Every time you sit down to make telephone canvassing calls, can you clear your mind of self-doubt? Concentrate on the goal of the moment and you will find that each new day will bring you to new heights in professional productivity and personal satisfaction.

Wrong ways and right ways to generate sales leads by telephone.

*T*here are four general areas that must be addressed in order for you to have a successful telephone lead generation program. The four areas are:

- **Presentation,**
- **Skills,**
- **List management and**
- **Preparation methods.**

If you don't want to throw away good money on staff, lists and telephone calls, let's take a closer look at how to manage your program.

PRESENTATION

At a recent dinner of esteemed members of the Connecticut IBM PC Users Group, some members were grousing at the expense of telephone sales people. You and I (and the rest of the civilized world) often take pot shots at people who cold-call us, because, for the most part, telemarketers often are living caricatures who foil themselves right from the first. See if you recognize any of these examples.

"Hello, Mr. Rosenzweig. How are you today."

This give-away opening line alerts me that I am about to be pitched by a total stranger who couldn't care less about my health or good fortune, but only cares about selling me something. How do I know? Easy. Nobody who knows me enough to care even the slightest bit about me ever starts his phone conversation by asking how I am today. My editor asks how business is doing, or when my next column will be ready. My sister says simply "What's new?" None of them ever utters those exact four words "How are you today?" Face it. We only get asked that specific four word question on the phone by complete strangers.

My response to "How are you today", depending on the number of unanswered callbacks to clients or relatives I have stacked up, is to answer "what's it to you, bub?" and play along to see how many other telemarketing errors I can uncover. In any case, the sales person has lost me through this gratuitous insincerity.

How about this one: "I am not trying to sell you anything, but..."

Oh, come on now! Who are you trying to kid? You don't know me from Adam, but you just want to inquire about my health? Why are telephone sales people afraid to admit what they do for a living? If your telemarketers are that ashamed of their craft, then you have failed at sales training, or failed at sales recruiting.

Here's one that I get at least once a month from the financial services community: "I don't have anything to sell you today, but we get great opportunities regularly. When a particularly good opportunity comes along, can I call you to pass it along?"

"Why not?" I reply. "I couldn't stop you this time."

Actually, asking for permission to call back at some time in the future is not a bad selling strategy, if you are only looking for prospects who actually believe that a salesman would call with no immediate offering. You have to judge the prospect's tolerance.

Not too long ago, somebody made this call to me that incorporated all of the above examples into the same opening: "Hello, Mr. Rosenzweig. How are you today? I am not trying to sell you anything, but the Sierra Club has arranged with our bank for you to obtain a MasterCard embossed with the pictures of endangered species... No, I don't know what the interest rate is, but the card looks great."

I guess that there are so many would-be sales people on the phone because, like direct mail marketing, it only takes a small percentage of yes responses to make money. Either that, or there are many more people who think they can be successful than those who will be. It's a lot like the current talk show phenomenon with Jay Leno, David Letterman, and Charlie Rose. They all think they have the right stuff, with new entries swelling the field almost daily. Daytime talk (I hear from others, having no time to turn on TV during business hours) is even worse.

Before you marvel at why this segment of the TV world is so overcrowded, consider that only one in ten life insurance sales people, or real estate people, or travel agents, or even candidates for public office, actually make a good living... and yet another 90% crowd their fields hoping for the brass ring.

So, if you want to develop a successful sales lead telemarketing presentation and become one of the 10% who make the other 90% look lame, do this:

1. Take a lesson in brevity from 30 second TV commercials. In fact, try to keep your opening to under 20 seconds.
2. Identify yourself and your mission without fanfare.
3. Plunge directly into a compelling benefit.
4. Ask a key question that moves the prospect's next decision from should he hang up to should he learn more from you.

Here is another quick and effective opening that we developed for the very crowded long distance business: "Hi. My name is Stan Rosenzweig. While many businesses spend up to 27 cents to send a one page FAX cross country, many of our clients spend as little as four cents. That's 85% less and these clients can't say enough nice things about us, the service is so good. Do you know if your company can benefit from our no-cost review of your telephone calling practices?"

Here, well within the critical first 20 seconds of the call we have identified ourselves and our mission, cited hot-button benefits for the prospect, asked the first of many questions that will include the prospect in a two way dialog, and tried to establish if this is, indeed, a genuine prospect worth pursuing.

When using the phone to develop sales leads and to improve your odds for that brass ring, you, or the people you train must plunge right in and get to the point. Your prospects will appreciate it more if you don't play stupid cat and mouse games and your appointment rate will improve.

SKILLS:

There are four skill areas that telemarketing people must be encouraged to never stop working on. They are listening, energy awareness, efficiency, and motivation and personal development.

1. Listening is most often discussed in selling seminars because of its great importance.

   Experienced and successful sales people know that most prospects have the information that holds the key to any sale and it is the sales person's job to find that key to unlock the sale.

   In telemarketing, good listeners keep a pen and paper in front of them at all times. They take notes during each call, focus the conversation on the objective of the call and encourage their prospect to reveal information that will facilitate the close, resulting in an appointment, a sale, or whatever your goal is.

2. Energy awareness is a term I use to identify the need to sound upbeat and positive on the phone.

The telephone is to selling what the radio is to drama. Since your audience cannot see you, you must be aware of and be able to project an energy level that keeps the prospect interested and enthusiastic about you. Telemarketers often place mirrors in front of callers to encourage them to smile and be conversational on the phone. It works to keep your callers energetic without their becoming obnoxiously aggressive.

3. Focus for efficiency is the skill to judge each call and to determine when to terminate it. Not all calls will end in a sale or an appointment no matter how good the telemarketer is. Your people should be trained in the art of determining when enough is enough and go on to the next call.

4. Motivation and personal development are the self improvement areas that are often overlooked. In the final analysis, there is just so much pumping up you can do for your staff before you wear yourself out. Therefore, it is important to institutionalize a procedure for telemarketers to study sales materials, go to classes and work on their own skills. This active quest for self improvement and its realization, is quite motivational and keeps your staff at a high readiness level.

LISTS AND PREPARATION METHODS

Your lead generation yield from cold calls will improve dramatically by careful list management and pre-call preparation. Firstly, divide your prospects into success categories. My categories are: a) existing customers, b) spheres of influence - referrals, c) total unknown.

For each category I decide how much softening up is needed prior to a call, and, again, I have three groups: a) no preparation needed, b) after a newsletter or mailed warm-up piece, c) timed to an event such as a national holiday or an impending price change.

Clearly, the "total unknown" group needs the greatest amount of warm up and I find it much more rewarding for telemarketers who are after this coldest business to follow up after a mailing. An alternative to a mailing is a pre-call call.

I remember how one of our suppliers once gave us a computer generated mailing list of potential prospects arranged by company size and potential need. This was a cold, cold list and the quality of the list was anybody's guess. So, I had a non-sales person call the listed names just to verify its accuracy, determine who the key decision makers would be for our products and ask the decision makers to participate in our marketing survey. Guess what? Most of them agreed.

We cleaned up the list, developed fine marketing intelligence on our target companies and gave the telemarketers ammunition that they could really get enthused about. We sent each prospect a letter thanking them for helping out in our survey, included sales material and followed up with sales calls.

Clearly, telemarketing is more than sitting people down at telephones with lists of numbers to call. It's also a marketing management issue that is often overlooked, but it is one that can prove richly rewarding.

10 Rules for successful Telemarketing.

*I*n the last lesson, we discussed wrong ways and right ways to generate sales leads by phone. We covered three of the worst common mistakes, three key tips for phone presentations, and how to improve in four skill areas. Lesson Five will cover how to script, for prospects who hide behind voice mail.

However, many of you have asked for a specific checklist to help you in your daily telemarketing training activities. We developed this list at a two-hour audience participation seminar at CompuExpo in Las Vegas. The seminar was only scheduled to last an hour and a half, but many of the 300 who attended asked to stay longer for this important selling subject.

Whenever I write about telemarketing, your response also indicates that this is an important subject for you, so, let's talk about the details of this telemarketing checklist that was developed by your peers, and how it can help you to improve the yield of your daily telephone selling efforts.

1. Never work without a script (but test that script for blunders). In the next lesson, we will discuss the three biggest telemarketing script blunders to avoid at all costs, as well as three tips for writing that killer script that works for your sales team. In Lesson Five, we will discuss how to prepare a script for leaving a message in a prospect's voice mail box, so you have enough material to tell HOW to craft your scripts.

   WHY should you do it? Because, the ability to use a script is one of the two great advantages telephoning has over face-to-face contact (the other is the conservation of travel time). When we were back in high school I had a history teacher, Mr. Miller, who resisted the consistent efforts of our class to persuade him to only give open book exams. "Real life doesn't afford you the opportunity for open book tests." Miller would say. "If you don't know it in your head, it won't do you any good."

   Well, you were wrong, Mr. Miller. Telemarketing is the ultimate open book test. All of your best points can be prepared ahead of time and you can refer to your notes as much as you wish... provided you are smart enough to HAVE notes.

2. Telemarket to a pre-mailed list. When I started out
   in the Phone Power department of New York
   Telephone a couple of decades ago, one of my jobs
   was to get our customers to make more phone calls.
   Back then, whenever we succeeded in teaching
   anyone how to profit from making more phone
   calls, we made more money, too, because, back then,
   there was only one phone company that would
   profit from the increased number of calls: ours. The
   entire telephone business was controlled by us (and,
   perhaps, gracious me, Lily Tomlin).
   During several years as a Phone Power trainer, I
   learned that we could get the trainees of our
   customers quickly up to speed by softening up
   their target lists with pre-call mailings. Then the
   telemarketers could phone as follow-ups to the
   mailings by saying something like "I am calling to
   follow up on the offer we made to you last week
   and to determine how we can modify it to meet
   your needs." The mail/phone one/two punch often
   proves irresistible.

3. When breaking in new material, a new offer, or new
   people, make calls to your LEAST LIKELY prospects
   first. Save your best prospects for your best efforts.
   You may start off with poor results in the first
   week, but your overall sales will be much higher.
   This is obvious when you think of it. When you
   break in new material, you are most likely to blow it
   because you are new to the presentation. If you
   practice on those who are least likely buy from

you anyway, who cares. When you get really good at your pitch, that's the time you want to talk to the prospect who can best use your product or service. That's why Broadway shows end up on Broadway after they've been to New Haven instead of before.

4. Get a hot button benefit out early, usually within the first 15 seconds of the call. If the prospect sees a benefit in speaking with you, he won't shut you down.

   Is there anyone in sales who doesn't know what a hot button benefit is? For the accountants among us, a hot button benefit is a dramatic announcement that makes the prospect literally jump up from his seat and shout "YES! YES!"

   In my own opening pitch, I gave this example: "While many businesses spend up to 27 cents to send a one page FAX cross country, our clients spend only four cents. That's 85% less."

   Here are a few additional hot button benefits that we use consistently (when they apply, of course):

- We can install your entire network and system in the time it takes others to complete the estimate.
- If you are not 100% satisfied with our consulting report, we will cancel our entire fee and you owe us nothing.
- We typically show Returns on Investment of 100% or more and break even within the first year.

To me, if the prospect does not react positively, or at least inquisitively to this kind of revelation, I think that it is time to move on to the next call and save my time.

5. Start fact finding ASAP to get the called party involved in the conversation. If you follow up the hot button benefit with a fact finding question, the prospect will let you know right then if he is qualified to be worth more of your time, if he can be sold and how you can best pursue the conversation.

Remember a conversation implies two way traffic, so don't hog the line. Slow down, listen and learn as much as the prospect will tell you about what he needs and how you can meet those needs.

6. Have a clear set of goals in mind for each call. This is not as simplistic as it sounds. Most salesmen think the goal of the call is to make a sale.

This is too broad. In fact, your call goals may be
to qualify prospects, to make appointments, to
determine if they are satisfied with existing service
(or if they hate you and are looking to change
suppliers), if they have other suppliers but are
open to new choices, etc.

You can wing it in a face to face meeting if you
want to, because there is a lot more personality
selling and relationship building when you are live
and in person. In telephone cold calling, however,
you are not unlike a taped TV commercial playing
to a football fan at half time who has a remote
channel changer in his hand. If you get off the
track... click.

7. Look in the mirror when you telemarket (If you
have a telephone operation, have a mirror on every
sales person's desk). Tape your conversations and
listen to them for clarity, personality, energy level,
friendliness, and helpfulness.

Become aware of the telephone image you project
and try not to sound boring, monotonous, or
intense. Ask yourself, would I like to speak to a
stranger who sounds like me? Lighten up. Smile at
yourself in your mirror when you are talking.
Make the call and the job fun and you will project
to the prospect someone worth talking to.

8. Have Internet e-mail and a fax machine handy and
use them often to answer prospect questions with
the service and speed of a CAN-DO company.

Sometimes prospects need to visualize your answers. Sometimes they just want to put off deciding, just when you start to feel that you are on a roll and want the momentum to continue.

When that happens, fax, or e-mail, your answers to prospect's questions and then call them back the same day, while everyone's juices are flowing and the subject is still fresh and you won't have to start all over again next week when you have been long forgotten.

9. Take lots and lots of breaks, but very short ones. Selling is a craft, but there is a lot of art to it. Art is creative and creativity needs to be humanized. Have soda and juice around for the troops to keep those vital juices flowing.

10. Create a happy, but competitive atmosphere. Maintain comparative charts on the wall. Prizes to the daily, weekly, monthly winners, etc., work wonders to keep the energy level high.

High energy is a key ingredient to successful telemarketing. Beware of frenetic, but not productive energy. Chaos does not succeed, but good natured competition results in an atmosphere of: Close, close, close.

In summary, here is that telemarketing checklist that you can use everyday to keep your new trainees, your old veterans and you focused on the basics for telemarketing success. Photocopy it out of this book and keep on your desk next to your phone:

1. Never work without a script.

2. Follow up a pre-mailed list.

3. When breaking in new material, a new offer, or new people, make calls to your LEAST LIKELY prospects first. Save your best prospects for your best efforts.

4. Get a hot button benefit out early.

5. Start fact finding ASAP: get the called party involved in the conversation. Remember, a conversation implies two way traffic.

6. Have a clear set of goals in mind for the call.

7. Look in the mirror, tape your conversations and review them. Be aware of your image. Don't be boring, monotonous, and intense. Lighten up. Smile. Make it fun.

8. Have e-mail and a fax machine handy. E-mail and FAX answers to prospect's questions and then call back the same day, while everyone's juices are flowing.

9. Take lots and lots of breaks, but very short ones. Have soda and juice around for the troops.

10. Create a happy, competitive atmosphere to keep the energy level high. Close, close, close.

Five more rules for successful telemarketing.

*H*ere is my sales person's challenge. First, I am going to sell you on doing something you don't want to do... require the use of prepared telemarketing scripts by you or your phone reps for all telemarketing calls. Next, I am going to give you five rules to follow in order to be a raging success at it.

If you are a telemarketer, using scripts will cause a great jump in your productivity and your income. If you manage a telemarketing group, coaching your flock in the professional use of scripting will make them all so much more effective. Your customers and prospects will be infected with a new exciting energy, which will excite your reps, and around and around.

You know, in the communication craft we are in, it's really easy to be misunderstood. Even I can be misunderstood, misread, misinterpreted. This scripting business is a classic case in point.

In the lesson you just read, I listed the 10 most important rules for telemarketing. Heading the list, at Number One, was "Never work without a script." That rule was followed by a detailed explanation about how, why and when to use telemarketing scripting to your best advantage without coming across to your callers like you were reading.

I had prepared that chapter as a column (as well as the chapter on telephone lead generation) from a series of field seminars on telemarketing I had conducted and I recycled the two resulting columns into subsequent sessions as handouts.

During our feedback, the question and answer segment of these seminars, some of you told me that you didn't like to use scripts because you didn't want your presentations to come across the telephone line sounding like you were reading. Reading from a canned sales pitch to prospects, of course, is awful. I never, ever told anyone to "read" to people when I talk about using scripts. In fact, you can go back and reread that chapter now to prove it.

This certainly proves that old selling rule that "it's not what you say, but what your prospect hears that matters." In this case, I agree that you shouldn't read to prospects, yet I still maintain that you should use a script. Unfortunately, "script" to many of you is the same as reading

That's not unlike the honest computer salesman who tells his prospect that one should always back up one's data in case of a hard drive failure and then loses the sale because the prospect figures that the salesman wouldn't bring it up unless his drives were unreliable.

So that we fully understand each other, let me set you straight on the distinction between dull and boring reading and using a script:

1. I am vehemently opposed to sales people reading their presentations over the phone. Reading material you don't really know is unprofessional, lazy and dumb. It doesn't work, it gets callers angry and it usually gets people to hang up on you. This is not part of the formula for success.

2. Scripting, on the other hand, is downright brilliant, if you take a moment to understand it and then learn how to do it right. Good scripting is appreciated by caller and called alike. It gets great responses because the caller is prepared, energetic and a veritable cornucopia of usefulness.

Think of the way movie and TV personalities use scripts to communicate with you. David Letterman and Jay Leno both use cue cards, not so they can read to you. They use them to store their carefully prepared ideas for quick reference and then use them as spring boards to catapult their fresh ideas and ad libs.

It is said that most of the funny and successful movies we see start with truly funny scripts, which lead to lots of new spontaneous material as a result of the actors playing off of each other.

In the great family hit "The Lion King" from Disney, two comedians whose names I probably will never remember were hired to read the parts of two animals who were minor characters, a hyena and a wart hog. The two actors read the parts and joked around a lot. They were so successful at getting into the material and embellishing it that the characters were elevated from minor to major.

Sure, professional entertainers wing a lot of it, but who really believes that you can make a commercially successful movie without a basically good script? It's the synergy between prepared material and freedom of expression that creates the excitement.

It's the same thing with telemarketing. Salesmanship, like acting, or comedy, requires spontaneity, timing and a command of your material. But, also, like acting and comedy, salesmanship requires a scripted blueprint and lots of rehearsal, as well.

The best sales people you can learn from are morning radio personalities who keep you tuned in day after day, but who make a living selling things. Believe me, these guys and gals couldn't make those big bucks if they didn't have whole libraries of scripted things to refer to.

They have stacks of commercials they must air to pay the rent. They have glib one liners stored up for lulls in the day. They have interesting news clips from the morning paper. They never think of going on the air live without an extensive stack of quick response materials to fall back on.

Thus, they always have something great to say and they are interesting to listen to. Are you always interesting to listen to? That's not what your kids say.

So, how does Leno and Letterman's preparation translate to you? Here are my five rules for you and your sales people to follow, just like the entertainment pros do, in order to keep fresh, spontaneous, vibrant and informative conversations going all day long:

Rule 1: Get every member of your telemarketing team to write out, in outline form, all of their best sales arguments for each and every product or service you sell. Don't have them write out full sentences and paragraphs... just outline notes for quick referral. Don't worry about spelling, either.

News flash: Spelling doesn't count on the phone.

Have them put each product or service on a separate page so you can have each pertinent page in front of you when you need it. Don't try to save paper. I know a sales team that keeps their scripts in loose leaf binders for quick flipping. Others keep theirs on desk top computers on separate "pages", by product.

Rule 2: Regardless of the medium, keep the bottom third of each page blank, or leave very wide margins so that your reps can add new responses as they think of them in the heat of battle. You know, sometimes the greatest sales responses just seem to pop out when you least expect them. If you write them down, you will have them to use again and again.

Rule 3: Rehearse. Rehearse. Rehearse. Have the reps try out your material at least three or four times seated in a comfortable chair at a desk or table with a cup of coffee... but with a mirror in front of each of them. Mirrors do wonders for your natural sound. Make sure everyone looks into the mirror when they practice.

Rule 4: Never, ever be satisfied with the material you have. Get into the habit of adding and changing all the time. I jot down notes wherever I happen to be, whenever I get a great thought or two. I don't mind forgetting a great joke about oral hygiene health in some Montana Aryan Nation compound, but run me through the wringer and hang me out to dry if I fail to record a great thought that I can use in business.

Even highly successful writers keep journals for the same purpose and Truman Capote got one of his biggest best sellers by making notes of his daily contacts with the stars. Telemarketers can amass a wealth of material from their own stars, their customers.

If you are using paper instead of computers, maybe you shouldn't be in telemarketing, but you should sell cars instead. But since you are, every week, see to it that the old scripts are retyped with the new hand written additions cleaned up and the stale, dated stuff thrown out.

Rule 5: Every couple of weeks, get your whole telemarketing group together for a swap meet to exchange the best responses of the month. Praise and give credit (if not outright cash) for the best show.

Here's how it works for me. First off, I recognize that I am getting older and everyone knows that there are two sure signs of aging. Memory loss is one, but I can't put my finger on the other right now.

No matter, because I keep my PC-based contact manager open for business all day long. This is a godsend for remembering all those little nuances about all of my daily telephone contacts and actually makes me more conversationally user-friendly than when I am presenting live and in person.

In addition to the contact information, I have at my desk all of the key points about all of the subjects that can possibly come up. I make sales calls, service calls, engineering calls and I respond to numerous telephone interviews from other writers, but I am never at a loss for a quick response.

I have finger-tip availability of comparative costs, comparative rate hikes and inflation rates, a full list of features of all products and services we provide, responses to the most asked questions about service and references, lots of really juicy stories about the industry and tidbits about competitors that would make the *National Enquirer* envious.

To sum up, scripting enables me to have at the ready all of the memory joggers I need to sound positively brilliant without pause, without stumbling, bumbling and coming up empty.

On most weekends, when I am in the process of being terribly urbane and witty at dinners and cocktail parties, I often find myself reduced to relying on my wonderful wife for background and fill. I know many of you, so you cannot say that you don't do the same. Well, what do you do during business hours when your wives and husbands are not around to bail you out?

You punt. That's what. Well now you don't have to. Just follow the rules of the live entertainment industry... follow the script:

1. Write an outline.
2. Keep the bottom third blank.
3. Rehearse, rehearse, rehearse.
4. Never, ever, be satisfied with the material you have.
5. Every couple of weeks, get together and swap best responses.

Telemarketing to a voice mailbox.

You and I have never met and I want to sell you something. Somebody gave me the lead and I am now going to call you. I am dialing your number, see?! It's ringing, but I really hope your secretary doesn't answer. I hate to have to explain everything about a cold, cold call to your secretary/security guard who takes great pride in shooting down salesmen.

In fact, if the truth be told, I really hope that your business is progressive enough to have a voice mail system installed, so I don't even have to talk to you.

WHAT? VOICE MAIL? HAVE I LOST MY MIND???

Buy any self-respecting salesman a beer and he'll tell you that the one sales nemesis in the modern world is VOICEMAIL. They all hate it. To hear your best reps tell it, voicemail has made it impossible to reach any-body and everybody anymore.

So why do I actually HOPE that you have voice mail? Simple. When voice mail answers my cold call, there is nobody to get between you and me until I have had my say. A "say" is not a conversation, to be sure, since YOU only get to listen, but listen you will, if I am prepared for this vital aspect of telemarketing. In other words, instead of being disgusted by voice mail systems, I implore you to learn to use them to your advantage and, before long, you'll have more good sales appointments than news media have Y2K stories.

Voice mail, you see, has solved the age-old problem of how to get past pest-call screening. Here's how it works:

Old way:
Ring, ring.
Attendant: "Notachance Purchasing Company. May I direct your call?
Us: Hello, is Mr. Nottoday in?
Attendant: He's on the phone. I'll give you his secretary.
Us: Oh, no, not his secretary! #@@%#@!!!
Attendant: I beg your pardon?

New way:
Ring, ring.
Attendant: "Notachance purchasing. May I direct your call?
Us: Hello, is Mr. Nottoday in?
Attendant: He's on the phone. I'll give you his secretary.
Us: Do you have voice mail? I only have to leave a message.
Attendant: I'll connect you.

TERRIFIC! We're in. We've gotten past that first big hurdle to any cold call. Now, how can we use this opportunity to make a living? Piece of cake.

Think of it. You're now in advertising. The next 60 seconds is your own personal sound bite. It's a radio commercial that is written, produced and starring you. The differences between this radio ad and a real one are:

1. Ads on the radio are heard by thousands. This one by only one.
2. Radio ads may not reach any prospects. This one does.
3. Airwaves cost real money. This ad is as free as the air.
4. Radio stations can be turned off. Voice mail messages rarely are.

Caveat: While your quarry indeed might be trapped into sitting through all you have to say, don't be stupid. A long, dull, long, rambling, long, pointless, long, long speech isn't the kind of thing to win friends and influence people with, is it?

Instead of winning the most boring pitch award, for these perfect advertising "time slots", do what the pros do:
- Establish the goals of your spot (usually it's a meeting or live conversation).
- Prepare a script ahead of time. Keep it brief, no more than a minute, or two.
- Include a reference (if possible), what you sell, REAL benefits of a meeting and your phone number.

- Rehearse your presentation. Time it. Record it and play it back. Don't wince and say you just can't believe it... you really do sound that bad.
- Rewrite the script and re-record it until it sounds actually good enough to play on a real radio, but don't play it to your audience. Stay live.

Here are two scripts that our office developed for when they encountered hard to get prospects with voice mail:

30 second, cold call, no reference, script:

This is Stan Rosenzweig of Office Technology Consulting. Like you, I am tired of having AT&T, MCI and other sellers constantly pounding down our door with dozens of different long distance plans.

It seems that all of these calling plans, like airline fares, were devised to be confusing and complicated, while all we really need is for the biggest and best long distance company to provide us with the lowest rate.

Continuing the airline analogy, I am like your travel agent. I have tariff knowledge that can minimize your daily costs that I would like to share with you.

Call me back. Let me know if you and I can benefit each other. I promise to make my case in less than ten minutes and I will send you a quality wallet calculator just for hearing me out. Please dial (203) 323-6070. I look forward to speaking with you.

30 Second, cold call, with reference, script:

This is Stan Rosenzweig of Office Technology Consulting. I was referred to you by Tom Smith at The Computer Clinic. Tom tells me that you are shopping for a new network specialist and that your present software is not performing as well as it could.

Tom knows that, for the past two decades, we have been known as the can-do company that maintains an exceptional price/performance ratio on all our projects. We are creative, responsive, available and we have exceptional references.

I look forward to learning more about your networking needs and to sharing a few thoughts with you as to how we can meet those needs while staying within your budget. I am available any morning next week, except Wednesday. Please dial (203) 323-6070. I look forward to our first meeting.

Notice that in the first script, because it is a cold, cold call, we need to get him to identify with us and provide an extra incentive to take action and not just erase the message. We do this with the familiar reference to the many other calls he's getting and with the free gift.

In the second script, our reference source gives us the opportunity to become more personal with the prospect and press more directly for an appointment, even though we have never met.

Not bad, huh? In both cases, we have bridged the gap with a complete stranger we have not yet had the opportunity to converse with... and may never have, if not for the new opportunity provided by voice mail.

Want to become a telemarketing powerhouse?

*F*ine. Do this: Keep the prospect involved, keep the message simple and keep repeating your message until you get the order, or you hear dial tone. You will make more money.

It used to be fashionable to use logical reasoning in everyday life. We talked about common sense. We taught reasoning in schools (and maybe still do for those who pay attention in class - a new minority, indeed).

Somewhere along the line, the world slid, ever so slowly, imperceptibly, to where sound bites have replaced cogent argument. "Newspeak" of "1984" has finally taken firm hold on us. For example, freedom is now defined by many as the unrestricted ability to sell machine guns and/or smoke until our last breath.

Does this present a marketing opportunity for you? Perhaps it does, if you can recognize when newspeak is being spoken by your competitors and can put the "de" back in debunk.

Let's perform a business school analysis of one current advertising phenomenon that we are all quite aware of: the constant bombardment to change our long distance company. Have you wondered how every phone company sells better service for lower rates?

Prime Time Live's Diane Sawyer wondered, too. On television, Ms. Sawyer exposed an apparent deceptive advertising practice that was said to be perpetrated equally by all three of the largest telephone long distance companies, AT&T, MCI and SPRINT.

This practice is in the form of an ad campaign that has been going on for years without being challenged. Perhaps, it's because the Davids of the world have lost the nerve to stand up to the Goliaths, while none of the big guys want to blow the whistle on each other, or themselves.

According to Ms. Sawyer, each company advertises that they will provide residence long distance phone service that is lower in cost than the other two. But, how can this be, she asks. How can they all be better and cheaper (See! My question, exactly!)?

The answer, she found, was in the unvoiced details. Ms. Sawyer showed America that these three telephone carriers collectively controlled a whopping 90% of the long distance market by applying a formula that always offers "new lower rates" without ever cutting revenues. Gosh! Them's statistics even Bill Gates could envy.

The winning long distance telephone formula of these giants, reported by Ms. Sawyer, was simply to NOT guarantee to keep those great rates from going up in a week or two. Thus, those "new lower rate" promotions could have been pre-planned by management, but not pre-announced to customers, in order to escalate the new accounts into a higher class of charges within a few months. You signed at the guaranteed lowest rate seven months ago, so your current rate is now above the guaranteed lowest rate of all of the big three today.

Back in the days when we thought things through, if a travelling salesman, like Professor Harold Hill in "The Music Man", had tried to flimflam us like that, the community would have tarred him, feathered him and run him out of town. Today, we see things through Alzheimer's glasses. We can't connect yesterday's promise with today's bill and, er, er... What's on Oprah?

I once received a phone call from a telemarketing rep from AT&T. It could just as easily have been a call from MCI Worldcom or SPRINT. This was a genuine call that begs to be used as a marketing lesson in how to train sales people for maximum effect in a world where people don't want the details.

We'll call the salesman Shaun. I take detailed notes on these calls (in a particular kind of proprietary shorthand which I can only read back with accuracy that resembles OCR circa 1986, but good enough for sales training).

Shaun: Hello Mr. Rosenzweig. My name is Shaun. How are you today? (You know, now, that this is the classic give-away of a cold call from a stranger).

Me: Great, Shaun. What can I do for you this fine day? (You know that I will always be polite to telemarketers, so that I can learn how well they are trained, so I can pick up a few new tricks along the road to pass along to you readers, so I can learn if they live nearby and if I can recruit them to sell for us).

Shaun: I am with AT&T. We monitor our lines for quality and I was doing a line check and found that you are no longer with AT&T and I am calling to invite you back.

Me (acting very alarmed): Are you telling me that even though I am not an AT&T customer, you monitor my lines?

Shaun (flustered): No, no. I didn't say that we monitor your lines. I said we monitor OUR lines. My supervisor listens in to see that I am doing a good job. If you come back to AT&T, we can give you a discount of 20%. That's better than MCI and the same as SPRINT, and if you are not happy within 90 days, we will switch you back at no charge.

In other words, salesmen like Shaun are supposed to tell me that his company is listening in on the conversation to assure that he only says what they approve of, but they found a way to have him relay that information in a way that would give me the idea that they were omnipotent, had their finger on MY pulse and could monitor MY lines for quality.

When I asked Shaun to tell me the cost per minute that his 20% would be discounted from, he said that the company policy was not to tell him, the salesman, but that it "was very competitive." I really didn't believe this, so, after Shaun had repeated his message several times and failed to convert me, he got his supervisor on the line.

Shaun's supervisor, whom we'll call Lisa for this discussion, also told me that she did not know AT&T's per minute rate, but volunteered, eventually, that it was somewhere in the neighborhood of "up to the mid 20's" (cents per minute), twice the rate we now pay. That didn't matter to Lisa because, even without knowing the actual rate, she said, "I bring back people every day!"

Boy, Lisa. If you ever decide to move to Connecticut and need a job... Yet, this is a $10 billion business, so wouldn't you think that the actual rate had at least a little to do with the decision?

No, said Lisa, and here's why. Firstly, long distance resellers often quote rates that are half of her company's, so getting into a rate war doesn't sell, a good lesson for anyone to learn. She then went on to make several *prima-*

facie sales arguments that were mighty convincing had I not been well schooled in the telephone business.

That didn't deter Lisa, who was prepared to sell so long as I was willing to keep talking... and keep listening (that's part of the lesson, folks). She told me that other services have "dirty" lines that don't send faxes at the full speed, costing more money by making the fax calls longer. She painted great word pictures.

"Our fax data goes through twice as fast as the other lines. It's like having the drain in the kitchen sink plugged so the water empties out slowly. Your fax is cut back to 4800 baud, which costs twice the price to send a fax." Like a true pro, Lisa never stopped trying to close the deal.

Fortunately, unlike most managers, I do know our fax and data throughput and Lisa's observations were just not correct in our case. Had I not been a telecom pro, however, I could not have refuted many of her points and she surely would have nailed me.

This lesson has little to do with the cost of phone calls, but a lot to do with research into the psychology of selling on the phone. The major long distance companies prove every day that if you can keep a conversation going long enough without the prospect hanging up, can engage the prospect in conversation, have a simple to understand message and can repeat your basic message enough times, you will make a lot of money. In Lisa's case, the simple message was that AT&T was simply better. That was her story and (to paraphrase Saturday Night Live's Colin Quinn) she was sticking to it.

The telephone business is not unlike many other businesses. In the computer business, for instance, the move by the biggest commercial software publishers is to lower the cost of products at point of sale, with back-end loaded customer-support costs.

Computer printer manufacturers sell $99 color printers. They follow up with replacement ink cartridges that sell for $25, but cost less that $1 to make. And as Diane Sawyer pointed out, nobody asks what will happen in three months.

Of course, if you want to bundle ethics with salesmanship, something I heartily endorse, prescribe and practice, it wouldn't hurt for YOU to bring it up... thus, pointing out, by their own omission, the moral failings of your competition.

Then, to amend the opening line of this lesson, you can prosper in telemarketing if you keep the prospect involved, keep the message simple, point out the strength of your sense of ethics and moral fiber and keep repeating your own message until you get the order.

A Few Final Thoughts.

*T*elemarketing is harder in some ways than direct face-to-face selling, because the prospect has no idea who he or she is talking to. On the other hand, telemarketing is easier and a lot more fun for the same reason. You can dress as you like, if at all. You can imagine yourself taller, shorter, thinner, stronger – it's all up to you.

But, no matter your physical appearance, telemarketing success, as with any sales, always comes down to these bottom line questions:

- How many orders did you get today?
- How much money did you make your company today?
- How much money did you make for yourself today?
- Did you do more business today than yesterday?
- Did you do more this week than last week?

I have prepared the six lessons in **Smart Telemarketing** to be pleasantly conversational, comfortable to read, easy to understand, and short enough so that you will be able to repeat each lesson, over and over, until, like practicing a musical instrument, you will become practiced enough to be able to play "without the music."

To get the most from this training, remember to keep the "pace" in "self-paced" and never stop reading and working on these lessons. Make it a habit to take **Smart Telemarketing** with you to lunch. Refer to it throughout the day. Learn these principal points and you will soon find that you are selling much more than you had ever expected.

As you get comfortable with the principles, you will begin to develop an inventory of useful scripts for any objection and situation.

You will no longer fear voicemail. You leave well-rehearsed commercials of 30 seconds to a minute, just for your audience of one.

When you reach a new prospect for the first time, you will be able to rattle off a well prepared, well rehearsed 20 second opening that will entice your prospect to spend more time on the phone with you.

Once you are in the conversation, you will be able to continue on until you land more business. I do hope you make lots of money as a result of these time-tested methods and examples.

Finally, please let me know how you are doing. Drop me a note, or an e-mail, from time to time, and tell me of your successes, or challenges. Perhaps, you will have a new idea that we can credit to you in a subsequent edition.

Best of luck.

Stan Rosenzweig

GIFT ORDER FORM (cut out and mail)

Make a list of the men and women you know who will thank you for decades to come for this simple act of kindness. Each book you order will be specially gift wrapped with a very tasteful card enclosed that says: *"I found this selling course quite useful and thought you would like a copy. (Your name)."*

Enclose your check in the amount of $9.00 for each gift-wrapped copy and we will waive the two-day, $3.20 postage, the $3.50 package cost and the $1.50 personalized greeting card. Or fill out and sign the MasterCard/Visa authorization (Connecticut residents must add 6% sales tax).

Number of books ordered: _____ Title(s):_____

Number times $9.00 each: _____

In CT add 6% tax: _____ Total enclosed, or charged: _____

MasterCard/Visa account: _____

Expiration date: _____

Name on card: _____

Signature: _____

Phone: _____ E-mail: _____

Show the gifts from: _____
                                    (print clearly)

Send gifts to:

1. _____

_____

_____

2. _____

_____

_____

3. _____

_____

For additional space, use other side, or photocopy.

For more than 10 copies, for corporate distribution, for quantity pricing and for on-site seminar information, call 1-203-323-6070, ext. 305, or click on http://www.salestipwebsite.com

mail or fax to 203-356-1770

cut along this line

(Fold here. Tape 3 sides if including check)

Name: _____

Company: _____

Street: _____

City, State, ZIP: _____

Place
Stamp
Here

To:

Emery Publishing
800 Summer Street, Suite 340
Stamford, CT 06901

ORDER FORM (cut out and mail)

Book Title	Quantity	Cost/copy	Total
Smart Selling Twenty lessons that have helped thousands to earn millions. How you can turn ordinary selling into extraordinary income.	_____	$29.95	_____
Smart Marketing Marketing builds more revenue than selling alone and it's easy to do. Learn the secrets of brand building, public relations, and more, with scores of tips, tricks and lessons that produce immediate results.	_____	$29.95	_____
Smart Telemarketing Get more people to say "yes, yes" on the phone without ever meeting you in person.	_____	$9.00	_____

Connecticut orders, add 6% sales tax: _____

Total included with your order, or charged: _____

Coming soon...
(check www.smart-selling.com for schedule)

Smart Management How you can use these powerful lessons of others to help you to build and lead a winning sales and management team. $29.95.

Smart Thinking Chicken soup may be good, but front line sales experience is better. How to use your own life experiences to reach success. $19.95.

Check enclosed: _____ Credit Card: _____

MasterCard/Visa account: _____

Expiration date: _____

Name on card: _____

Signature: _____

Your shipping address (no P.O. box for UPS)

Name: _____

Company: _____

Street address: _____

City: _____ ST: _____ ZIP: _____

Phone: _____ E-mail: _____

For more than 10 copies, for corporate distribution, for quantity pricing and for on-site seminar information call 1 (203) 323-6070, ext. 305, or click on http://www.smart-selling.com

cut along this line ✂ mail or fax to 203-356-1770

(Fold here. Tape 3 sides if including check)

Name: _____

Company: _____

Street: _____

City, State, ZIP: _____

To:

Emery Publishing
800 Summer Street, Suite 340
Stamford, CT 06901

READER RESPONSE FORM

(cut out and mail back. We will respond with a suitable token of appreciation.)

Dear Stan:

I have just finished this course, **Smart Telemarketing**, and I have the following questions, suggestions and/or comments to share with you for your next edition.

Your thoughts here (then fold the page in half and tape it, stamp it and mail it right back to us):

_____

_____

_____

_____

_____

_____

_____

_____

_____

_____

_____

_____

_____

_____

_____

Phone: _____ E-mail: _____

cut along this line ✂ mail or fax to 203-356-1770

(Fold here. Tape 3 sides if including check)

Name: _____

Company: _____

Street: _____

City, State, ZIP: _____

To:

Emery Publishing
800 Summer Street, Suite 340
Stamford, CT 06901